PIANO 300

Celebrating Three Centuries of People and Pianos

Cynthia Adams Hoover

Patrick Rucker

Edwin M. Good

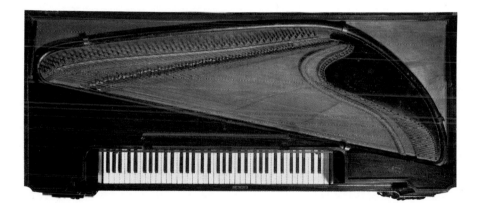

Compiled from the Exhibition Produced by the
National Museum of American History at the
Smithsonian International Gallery

March 9, 2000–October 21, 2001

National Museum of American History, Behring Center, Smithsonian Institution
and NAMM–International Music Products Association

© 2001 by The National Museum of American History, Behring Center, Smithsonian Institution
and NAMM-International Music Products Association.
All rights reserved.

PIANO 300: *Celebrating Three Centuries of People and Pianos*
Compiled from the exhibition produced by the National Museum of American
History at the Smithsonian International Gallery, March 9, 2000–October 21, 2001

Designer: Debra Naylor, Naylor Design, Inc.

ISBN 0-929847-08-3

Manufactured in the United States of America

front cover: Detail, square piano by Alpheus Babcock for William Swift, Philadelphia,
1833–1837. Babcock's invention of the iron frame was one of the signal American contributions to the development of piano design. SI photograph by Robert Lautman

back cover: Detail from the soundboard of the 1850 square piano by Jonas Chickering, Boston.
For further views, see pages 26–27. SI photograph by Robert Lautman.

CONTENTS

LENDERS TO THE EXHIBITION

Baldwin Piano Company

Horace Clarence Boyer

Cathedral Church of St. John the Divine, New York City

Michael A. Cummings

George and Kathryn Epple

Luvenia A. George

Robert Gilson

Edwin M. Good

Marilyn and Calvin Gross

International Piano Archives at the University of Maryland

Irving S. Gilmore Music Library at Yale University

Brian Jensen

Library of Congress

Museo Nazionale degli Strumenti Musicali, Rome

National Portrait Gallery

The Pierpont Morgan Library

Rosemary Regan

Patrick Rucker

The Schubert Club Museum of Musical Instruments

Frederick R. Selch

Smithsonian Institution Libraries

M. Steinert & Sons, Boston

Steinway & Sons

Charles Timbrell

Raymond A. White

ACKNOWLEDGMENTS

PIANO 300 was made possible by a generous leadership gift from NAMM—International Music Products Association, and gifts from Piano Manufacturers Association International, Music Educators National Conference, and The Irving Caesar Lifetime Trust. Additional support was provided by the Smithsonian International Gallery, Alitalia Airlines, The Friends of Music at the Smithsonian, The Jerome and Dorothy Lemelson Center for the study of Invention and Innovation, Mondial Designs, Ltd., The Smithsonian Institution Educational Outreach Fund, The Smithsonian Women's Committee, and US Airways.

In addition to their material support of *PIANO 300*, a number of individuals associated with these patron organizations played major roles in making the piano's tercentenary a national celebration. At NAMM, Joe Lamond and Larry Linkin early grasped the project's potential; without their steadfast backing there would have been no *PIANO 300*. Bruce A. Stevens, Terry Lewis, Brian Chung, Dennis M. Houlihan, Henry Z. Steinway, and Donald W. Dillon, all of PMAI, offered sage advice and put the significant resources of their respective companies at the project's disposal. Mike Blakeslee and his colleagues at MENC developed and distributed the curriculum kits that immeasurably enhanced *PIANO 300's* national outreach.

The exhibition was produced by the National Museum of American History, Behring Center, Spencer R. Crew, Director, in collaboration with the Smithsonian International Gallery, Smithsonian Productions, Smithsonian Office of Exhibits Central, and Smithsonian Office of Information Technology, and in cooperation with the Library of Congress–Music Division and Museo Nazionale degli Strumenti Musicali, Rome. The staff of the Smithsonian International Gallery—Anne R. Gossett, Lori Dempsey, and Lakshmi Kinger—were indefatigable in their efforts to assure a thoroughly professional and stylish presentation.

Two planning conferences at the National Museum of American History helped develop the scope of the project and brought a variety of ideas and perspectives to the exhibition's intellectual content. The first of these was held January 24–26, 1997, and included Mike Blakeslee, Eileen T. Cline, Lynn Edwards, Albert Fuller, William Garlick, Gene Gaudette, Maria Guralnik, Marshall B. Hawkins, John Koster, Terry Lewis, Randy Knee, David Lamoreaux, Jon Newsom, James Parakilas, Trevor Pinch, Sandra Rosenblum, Charles R. Suttoni, Frank Trocco, Barbara Wing, Thomas and Barbara Wolf, and Robert Wyatt. The second, focusing on the piano in the 20th century, took place December 3–4, 1998, and included Horace C. Boyer, Dje Dje Jacqueline Cogdell, Tom Constanten, Dennis Houlihan, Richard J. Howe, Michael Kovins, Joe Lamond, Donald Manildi, Trevor Pinch, and Edward Rothstein.

The exhibition curators were assisted in script development by two expert educators, Marcia Daft and Luvenia A. George, while editor Rosemary Regan rendered countless arcane concepts intelligible to the general audience. Daniel B. Murphy and Yachin Lee of Production Research and Design Group, Ltd., Fairfax, Virginia, designed the exhibition, and two gifted project managers, Patrick Ladden and Marion Gill, saw that it opened to the public on time and on budget. The exhibition was fabricated by Omar Wynn and the production staff at NMAH; Jonathan Zastrow created the action models. Thomas Bower, Stacey Kluck, and Beth Richwine provided invaluable expertise in assembling and preparing the objects. Publicity was coordinated by Valeska Hilbig and events were managed by Arlene Fenlon. Howard Bass and Susan Mond Carpenter produced the programs that enabled the public to hear the pianos.

PIANO 300's two PBS specials and the exhibition video were produced by Smithsonian Productions, Paul B. Johnson, Karen Loveland, Wesley Horner, John Paulson, and James Arntz, producers. The performance gala, *Piano Grand! A Smithsonian Celebration* was co-produced by Maryland Public Television, John Potthast, producer. The documentary, *People and Pianos: 300 Years*, was co-produced by EuroArts Music GmbH, Leipzig, Paul Smaczny and Klaus Wischmann, producers. James Parakilas edited the companion volume, *Piano Roles: Three Hundred Years of Life with the Piano* (Yale University Press) containing contributions by fifteen scholars. Mignon Erixon-Stanford created and maintained the Piano300.org website. Jane Freundel Levey edited the book *Piano 300: Celebrating Three Centuries of People and Pianos.*

The action of the Erard grand piano, 1854 (above). The Erard grand was the centerpiece of a *Piano 300* exhibition platform (right) dedicated to "The Romantic Superstar."

SI photographs by Robert Lautman, Richard Strauss & Terry McCrea.

The Romantic Superstar

PREFACE

After the Civil War, a German immigrant named Hugo Worch opened a music dealership in Washington, D.C. Worch was so grateful to his adopted country that he began collecting instruments illustrating the development of piano making in the United States and later added European keyboards. Before World War I, Worch began donating his extensive collection to the Smithsonian Institution. Of the roughly 5,000 artifacts that compose the musical instrument collections of the Smithsonian's National Museum of American History, some 300 are keyboards, and more than 180 of these are pianos. Many of the instruments owe their preservation as part of a national collection to the vision of Hugo Worch.

Given the breadth of this piano collection, it seemed appropriate that the Smithsonian would mount *PIANO 300*, a large-scale exhibition to coincide with the tercentenary of the piano's invention. Certainly few instruments can claim a more dominant and pervasive role in Western culture. In fact the story of the piano provides a unique index to many areas of inquiry within the history of our culture. Its sophisticated technologies of design and manufacture carry us from the craftsman's workshop to huge, highly automated factories. The case itself reflects shifting tastes in furniture and cabinet making, almost decade by decade. The piano's sheer size and weight made it the dominant article of furniture in many households, where pianos functioned as home-entertainment centers. There families and friends gathered to make music, children were taught, and courtship rituals were enacted. Indeed during the nineteenth century, the piano had an important elevating influence on the status of women who mastered it.

For most of its three centuries, the piano has inspired composers and performers to write and play a vast terrain of literature as

Washington piano dealer Hugo Worch (1855-1938), seen here at an 1860s Kuhn and Ridgeway (Baltimore) harp piano, began donating his piano collection to the Smithsonian in about 1910. Worch's pianos, including this harp piano, form the core of the museum's collection of more than 180 pianos.

Pictured on the PIANO 300 banner is the Steinway & Sons grand piano designed by Walter Dorwin Teague for the 1939 New York World's Fair. *PIANO 300*, scheduled to close on March 4, 2001, was extended twice. At right, Brian Jensen applies the second extension announcement to the exhibition banner outside the S. Dillon Ripley Center at the Smithsonian Institution.

SI photograph by Robert Lautman; photograph by Debra Naylor.

rich and varied as that written for any musical instrument. Here, too, change is the only constant—the pianos played by Mozart and Clementi were very different from those known to Chopin and Liszt, let alone the ones used by Tatum and Bartók. And perhaps more than any other musical instrument, the piano has achieved an iconic status quite apart from its function as a producer of sound. Hollywood movies of the twentieth century are rich with these allusions, where the piano evokes status and chic, showbiz panache, romance, or nostalgia. When the piano, that marvel of mechanical and artistic achievement, is dropped from the top of a building to smash into thousands of parts below, it seems a hilarious assault on culture itself. Throughout it all, the piano has progressed slowly around the globe, from its origins in Italy, throughout Europe and its colonies, to Asia, where most pianos are made today.

Because the piano stands at the confluence of so many streams of human endeavor—invention, manufacture, artistic achievement, economic activity, education—the creation of an exhibition on a topic at once so circumscribed and far reaching meant that much had to be excluded. Pride of place belonged to the Smithsonian's instruments, set in context through images, text, related objects, and musical examples. *PIANO 300* contained 27 pianos and keyboards, of which only four were borrowed. In choosing the pianos to display, the curators chose the most important and interesting instruments in the Smithsonian collection that would illustrate these episodes in the life story of people and pianos. During its 18-month run, the exhibition welcomed more than 330,000 visitors. An exhibition video, along with two PBS television programs produced by Smithsonian Productions, amplify themes of the exhibition. The exhibition closed in October 2001 after being extended twice. This book captures its highlights and in so doing offers a quick history of the piano's development.

INVENTION

hree hundred years ago in Florence, Italy, the piano made its first sounds, and the world of music received its most versatile instrument. Bartolomeo Cristofori (1655–1732) invented a keyboard instrument by 1700 that made strings vibrate when small leather-covered hammers struck them. His new mechanism allowed the player to control the loudness and softness of music through the finger's pressure on the key.* Cristofori's new instrument was called at first *gravecembalo col piano et forte* or keyboard instrument with soft and loud. The name was soon shortened to *fortepiano* or *pianoforte,* and later to just piano.

Employed by Ferdinando, Grand Prince of Tuscany, to make and repair harpsichords for the vibrant musical activity at the Medici court, Cristofori demonstrated remarkable inventiveness with the piano as well as unique harpsichords and clavichords. During the 1720s, some of his pianos were purchased for the royal court of Portugal and soon were taken to the royal court of Spain, where composer Domenico Scarlatti knew them.

By the 1730s, the German instrument maker Gottfried Silbermann was experimenting with Cristofori's ideas. Some of his pianos were purchased by Frederick the Great for the Prussian court, where no less a musician than Johann Sebastian Bach played them in 1747. The costly and individually hand-crafted new instruments still resided among the highest ranks of European society.

---

* The introduction of hammers distinguished the piano from the harpsichord and clavichord. The harpsichord made its sound by plucking the strings, and the player could not alter the loudness of any note. Its sound was big enough to be used with orchestras and in operas. The simpler clavichord sounded when a brass strip at the back of the key touched the string. It could vary its dynamic, but its loudest sound was quite soft.

This grand piano, made by Cristofori in 1722, is the second oldest of three known pianos made by the inventor of the piano. The instrument was lent to Piano 300 by the Museo Nazionale degli Strumenti Musicali in Rome. For technical details on this and other instruments in the exhibition, please see the Appendix.

SI photograph by Hugh Tallman.

Inventor Bartolomeo Cristofori (1655–1732) is seen next to a keyboard instrument, holding a drawing of a piano action. The painting, the only known Cristofori portrait, belonged to Staatliches Institut für deutsche Musikforschung in Berlin but was lost or destroyed during World War II.

Courtesy of Tony Bingham.

This page from a 1700 inventory of instruments of the Medici Court—where Cristofori served the Grand Prince of Tuscany—describes an "Arpicimbalo [Italian for large keyboard instrument] by Bartolomeo Cristofori of new invention, which produces piano [soft] and forte [loud]." A few lines later, it mentions "martelli [hammers] that produce soft and loud," confirming that the Arpicimbalo was a piano.

From Archivio di Stato, Florence, courtesy of Stewart Pollens.

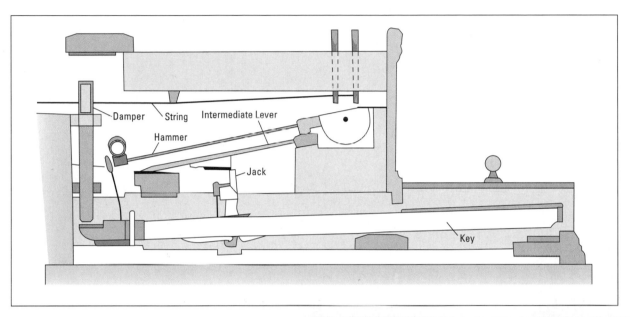

In the action by piano inventor Bartolomeo Cristofori 1726 piano, the key moves the jack up against the intermediate lever, which propels the hammer to the string, while the end of the key pushes the damper up from the string. The principle of the piano is that the hammer flies free to the string and the action's leverage gives the player control of the speed and therefore the loudness.

Drawing by Debra Naylor.

The hand of Barbara Wolf, who tuned many of *Piano 300's* early pianos, plays the 1722 Cristofori keyboard, revealing the delicacy of the working parts. Notice especially that the hammer is a small block of wood with a deerskin pad on top.

SI photograph by Hugh Tallman.

Cristofori worked for a time in the Uffizi Palace in Florence, seen at left in an engraving of 1744, but later preferred to work at home. The view looks through the palace to the high tower of the Palazzo Vecchio and the familiar dome of the Duomo (cathedral).

From Giuseppe Zocchi, *Views of Florence,* 1744, courtesy of Beinecke Rare Book and Manuscript Library, Yale University.

Most of Johannes Zumpe's little square pianos graced wealthy homes like that of *George, 3rd Earl Cowper with his Wife and the Family of Charles Gore* (1775), painted by Johann Zoffany. The instrument in the painting is practically a twin of the one in the exhibition (inset) made by Zumpe and Gabriel Buntebart of London, 1770. For more than a century square pianos were the instrument of choice for amateurs in North America.

Painting courtesy of the Paul Mellon Collection, Yale Center for British Art, Yale University; SI photograph by Hugh Tallman.

EARLY STAGES: THE AMATEUR PLAYER

When small pianos began to be designed and built in the 1760s, they too went into aristocratic and wealthy homes. Johannes Zumpe, a German immigrant to London, designed what has come to be called a "square" piano (actually rectangular). He advertised it to "the Nobility and the Gentry" and soon had more orders than he could fill. Zumpe's square pianos were as popular in France as in England, and other English and French instrument makers tried their hands at the design during the 1770s. These little instruments were primarily for private entertainment in homes. Wealthy amateurs, mostly women, favored these pianos for learning to play the easier dances, sonatas, and songs that composers and publishers found profitable.

John Behrent, a German immigrant to Philadelphia, was America's earliest known piano maker. His advertisement appeared in the March 13, 1775, *Dunlap's Pennsylvania Packet*. When John Adams inspected Philadelphia's defenses that year, he wrote that Michael Hillegas, a music dealer and treasurer of the Continental Congress, talked "perpetually of the Forte and Piano."
Courtesy of the Library of Congress.

James Hewitt (1770–1827), one of early America's important composers, wrote *The Battle of Trenton* (New York, 1797) to mark one of George Washington's important Revolutionary War victories. During this period, piano pieces that musically described the course of a battle with sounds of marching soldiers, galloping cavalry, cannons, cries of the wounded, and victory processions were very popular.
Courtesy of the Library of Congress.

Alexander Reinagle (1756–1809), seen here circa 1800, was a leading pianist and composer working in America. He organized and led concerts, wrote theater music and sophisticated sonatas for the piano, and taught students—one of whom was George Washington's granddaughter Nelly Custis.
From Oscar Sonneck, *Early Opera*, 1915; courtesy of Smithsonian Institution Libraries

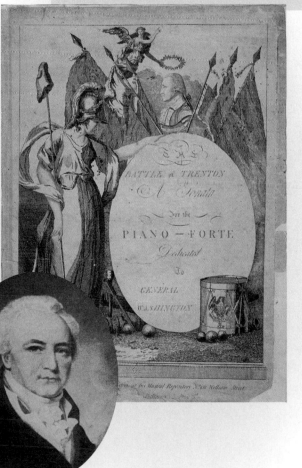

JOHN BEHRENT, JOINER and INSTRUMENT MAKER, living in Third-street continued, in Campington, directly opposite Coates's Burying-ground, HAS just finished for sale, an extraordinary fine instrument, by the name of PIANO FORTE, of Mahogany, in the manner of an harpsichord, with hammers, and several changes: He intends to dispose of it on very reasonable terms; and being a master in such sort of work, and a new beginner in this country, he requests all lovers of music to favour him with their custom, and they shall not only be honestly served, but their favours gratefully acknowledged, by their humble servant, JOHN BEHRENT.

EARLY STAGES: THE RISE OF THE PUBLIC PERFORMER

The piano was making its way into concert life, and by the 1780s, as more composers wrote for the piano, two centers of innovative piano design emerged in Vienna and London. Wolfgang Amadeus Mozart had an outstanding career in Vienna as a virtuoso, playing on small grand pianos with very subtle, responsive actions and the light, graceful tone that typified Austrian and South German instruments and piano playing. In London, the Italian-born Muzio Clementi played the larger English grand pianos that featured more strings, a heavier action mechanism, and bigger tone.

This grand piano by Louis Dulcken of Munich, made circa 1788, has the region's delicacy and silvery tone. Mozart and Beethoven performed on similar small, elegant instruments. Such pianos offered deep, bassoon-like low tones; warm middle tones; and bright, flute-like top tones. Players moved knee-levers beneath the keyboard to lift the dampers and sustain the sound.

SI photograph.

In the Dulcken grand's action, the tail of the hammer catches in the notch behind it, and the hammer pivots up to the string. Notice that the small, leather-covered hammers strike toward the player; in today's pianos, they strike away. The action is very light and responsive, capable of subtle phrasing.

Drawing by Debra Naylor.

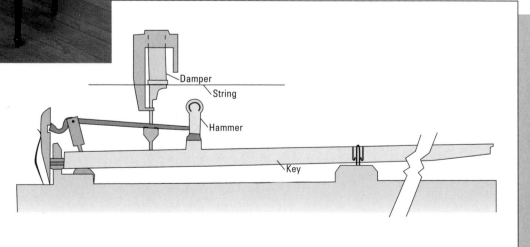

Damper
String
Hammer
Key

Like other English pianos, this 1794 grand piano by John Broadwood & Sons of London has a louder, more resonant tone than German and Austrian instruments and has more notes. Pedals instead of knee levers sustain and vary the tone quality.

SI photograph by Robert Lautman.

In the English grand piano action, the key pushes up the jack, which propels the hammer to the string. The jack catches on the let-off button and then moves away from the descending hammer butt. The English action is heavier than the Viennese to activate larger hammers. It was the basis of the more developed action now used in grand pianos.

Drawing by Debra Naylor.

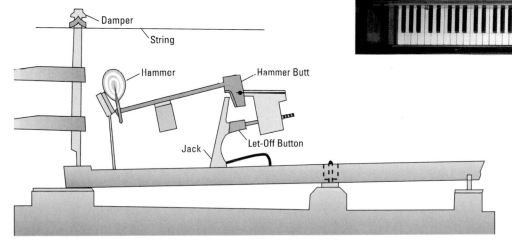

Damper
String
Hammer
Hammer Butt
Jack
Let-Off Button

Composer and pianist Wolfgang Amadeus Mozart (1756–1791) plays a duet with his gifted sister Nannerl as their violinist father Leopold listens beneath a portrait of their mother, circa 1780. Mozart, the most brilliant player of Austrian pianos, began his astounding career at the age of four, touring Europe with his family and playing before royalty and crowds of admirers.

Engraving after the painting by Johann Nepomuk della Croce, courtesy of Internationale Stiftung Mozarteum, Salzburg, Austria.

Muzio Clementi (1752–1832), seen here in an engraving by Thomas Hardy, was Mozart's chief rival as a pianist. An important composer, Clementi was a manufacturer—and promoter—of the English piano. He created a style of playing tailored to the distinctive qualities of English pianos, their sturdiness of tone and capacity for brilliant effects.

Courtesy of the Music Library, Yale University.

This handwritten manuscript of Mozart's Piano Concerto in C major, K. 467 (1785) shows that his penmanship was like his music: clear and elegant.

Courtesy of the Pierpont Morgan Library, New York.

THE ROMANTIC SUPERSTAR

s the nineteenth century began, concert pianos were expanding in size, power, and brilliance. Ludwig van Beethoven (1770–1827) witnessed the growth of the instrument from 61 keys, like Mozart's piano, to 78 keys in his last instrument. By the late 1820s, a few instruments had 85 keys, almost the full modern range (88 keys), and Sébastien Erard in Paris had invented his "repetition" action, which later grew into the modern grand piano action. In response to these trends, piano makers began to introduce iron into the piano's frame to make it louder and more stable.

As the European and American middle classes became more affluent, musical events were becoming popular entertainment. New concert halls could hold larger audiences than the few hundred of prior years. Orchestras grew in size, and instruments were becoming louder and more brilliant. The cutting edge of piano technology moved to Paris, where makers like Erard and Pleyel provided Romantic virtuosos such as Franz Liszt, Frédéric Chopin, Clara Wieck Schumann, and Marie Moke Pleyel with pianos that matched their technical and expressive achievements.

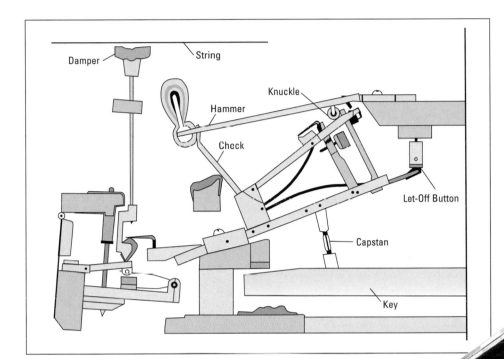

Damper — String — Knuckle — Hammer — Check — Let-Off Button — Capstan — Key

Sébastien Erard improved the grand piano with the 1821 "repetition" action. The jack is pushed up against the knuckle on the hammer shank, which propels the hammer to the string. As the jack moves up, it is forced sideways by the let-off, so that the descending shank does not hit it, but the hammer head is caught by the check.

Drawing by Debra Naylor.

In the 1850s, the Erard grand piano, manufactured in both Paris and London, was the state of the art in piano making. This 1854 instrument, bought in London by Queen Victoria for Prince Albert, spent most of its life in Balmoral Castle. The Erard was a favorite of Franz Liszt from the time he first came to Paris in 1823. Romantic virtuosos exploited the new instruments with techniques creating long, singing lines, vibrant colors, and elaborate figurations emulating operatic and orchestral sounds.

SI photograph by Eric Long.

Reminiscence of Liszt, this remarkable 1840 painting by Joseph Danhauser (left), symbolizes the Romantic movement. Franz Liszt gazes at a bust of Beethoven while playing a Conrad Graf piano (the Viennese maker Graf commissioned the painting). Liszt's mistress, Countess Marie d'Agoult, swoons at his feet, and leaders of the Romantic movement listen. Clockwise are writers George Sand and Alexandre Dumas père, seated; poet Victor Hugo, standing; violinist Niccolò Paganini; and composer Gioacchino Rossini.

Courtesy of Preussicscher Kulturbesitz, Berlin.

Liszt's dazzling keyboard style, exploiting the full range of the piano's registers, is evident from these manuscript pages of his Concerto No. 1 in E-flat major (1855). In Liszt's hands, the piano came to emulate the sonorities of the orchestra.

Courtesy of the Library of Congress, SI photograph by John Tsantes.

This locket (inset) containing the hair of Liszt and pianist/composer Anton Rubinstein (1829–1894) was given by the noted teacher Theodore Leschetizky (1830–1915) to his pupil Ossip Gabrilowitsch (1878–1936), who married Mark Twain's daughter. The brown hair is Rubinstein's, the white hair, Liszt's.

Courtesy of Raymond A. White, SI photograph by Hugh Tallman.

The Hungarian Franz Liszt (1811–1886), possibly the greatest pianist of all time, took piano playing to an unparalleled level in a 65-year career and more than 600 compositions. Beginning in 1839, he pioneered the solo recital. Liszt aroused powerful emotions in his fans, just as many rock stars do today. At his concerts, like the 1842 Berlin performance illustrated here, women fainted and men wept. Some pelted the stage with flowers and jewelry.

Caricature by Adolf Brennglass, courtesy of Märkisches Museum, Berlin.

Polish-born Frédéric Chopin (1810–1849), the poet of the piano, was as brilliant as his contemporaries. But temperament and fragile health led him to prefer small salons to concert halls. Chopin was in great demand as a teacher by Parisian high society. At right, he admonishes the singer Pauline Viardot-Garcia, "That's the Liszt way of playing! You mustn't play like that when accompanying the voice."

Drawing by Maurice Sand (1844), courtesy of Michele Maurois.

Louis Moreau Gottschalk (1829–1869), born in New Orleans and pictured above, was the first American musician to win international fame and a passionate following with his showmanship, including his trademark rapid-fire "tremolo," caricatured here. After European study and concertizing successes, he made a sensational New York debut in 1853. Wherever he performed, admiring young women threw themselves at his feet. He organized "monster" concerts with 50 to 70 pianos on stage to perform his compositions.

Caricature by Henrique Fleuss from *A Semana Illustrada* (Rio de Janeiro, Brazil, July 4, 1869), courtesy of S. Frederick Starr; lithograph by Sarony and Knapp, ca. 1860, courtesy of National Portrait Gallery.

A small man who probably suffered from tuberculosis, Chopin lacked the sheer physical power of his heaven-storming virtuoso contemporaries, Liszt and Sigismond Thalberg. Instead, Chopin played with infinite varieties of nuance and touch within a limited dynamic range. His personal elegance and refinement is captured in this portrait by Ary Scheffer (1847).

Courtesy of Dordrechts Museum, Dordrechts, Netherlands.

Powerful prejudices against women as public performers long kept many women pianists from concert careers. But by 1830, a few extraordinary women had established themselves as leading pianists. Marie Moke Pleyel (1811–1875), seen at left, triumphantly toured Europe and Russia, captivating both Liszt and Chopin with her playing. Beginning a concert career at the age of nine, Clara Wieck Schumann (1819–1896), above, became one of Europe's pre-eminent pianists, especially as interpreter of the music of her husband, Robert Schumann.

Reproduction of Pleyel lithograph by Jacolin, after a drawing by Marie-Alexander Aloph (circa 1830), courtesy of Bibliothèque Nationale, Paris; reproduction of Schumann lithograph by J. Giere (1835), courtesy of Robert-Schumann-Haus, Zwickau, Germany.

Chopin's elegantly written manuscript of the Impromptu in G-flat major, op. 51 (1842), is typical of his richly crafted, deeply felt, and usually small-scale masterpieces. His "singing style" of piano-playing was inspired by the expressiveness of great Italian opera singers.

Courtesy of the Library of Congress, SI photograph by John Tsantes.

PIANOS AT HOME: THE PIANO GIRLS

The desire for pianos in nineteenth-century homes stimulated makers to new space-saving designs. Prosperous European homes might have large uprights—grand pianos set on their heads. In England they were shaped like cabinets or bookcases, and Germany and Austria saw characteristic curved shapes, some called "giraffes." Experiments in small upright instruments by makers such as the English Robert Wornum and the French Henri Pape made good instruments available to more modest homes. Very large uprights died out within a few decades, but small uprights ("pianinos," the Europeans called them) continued in favor throughout the century. Americans preferred square pianos, which stood up well to the North American climate. Although Europeans had abandoned them by 1860, many American makers built ever larger square pianos until the end of the century.

Music in European and American homes was the domain of women throughout the nineteenth century. Playing the piano was seen as a necessary female accomplishment along with other household tasks. In period images of piano-playing in homes, it is typically a woman who is seated at the instrument. Women were an extraordinarily important force in passing on musical interest and participation to children.

Americans preferred the square piano like this 1850 model (left and above) by Chickering & Sons of Boston for their homes until the 1870s, when the upright came into fashion. But square pianos had grown well beyond the size of the little Zumpe of 80 years before. The Chickering now had 85 keys (the Zumpe had 60), and a decorative iron frame providing strength and stability to keep the instrument in tune. Squares like this probably cost about $350. In 1850, the firm made about 10 percent of all American pianos and would dominate U.S. manufacturing for some time to come.

SI photographs by Robert Lautman.

While the "Portable Grand Pianoforte" built in Philadelphia in 1801 by John Isaac Hawkins (1772–1854) may have been portable (it has handles on the side), it was definitely not grand. This very early small upright was the first with strings to extend to the floor. Other features show Hawkins's ingenuity: the keyboard folds up into the case, shutters below open to increase volume, and iron bars brace the soundboard. Thomas Jefferson owned one, but sent it back, complaining that it would not stay in tune.

SI photograph.

This upright giraffe piano made by André Stein of Vienna around 1810 takes up little floor space but gives a grand piano sound. Stein was part of an important dynasty of piano makers. His father Johann Andreas perfected the Viennese action, and his sister Nannette Streicher was one of the few women who succeeded in piano manufacture. Note the six pedals. Giraffes were made during a European fad for modifications of piano tone.

SI photograph by Hugh Tallman.

A clever solution to the space problem was this sewing table piano, made in Germany or Austria circa 1820–1840. Appearing to be a side table when closed, its lid opens to reveal a handsome inlay and mirror, sewing compartments with implements and places for material and thread, and, somewhat incidentally, a small, 4-octave keyboard. With this instrument, a girl could practice some of the "accomplishments" required for womanhood: needlework and playing the piano (in addition to dancing and singing).

SI photographs by Eric Long.

In *The Family Concert* (circa 1845), by an unknown artist in the northeastern United States, a prosperous middle-class family reveals contemporary family values. The eldest daughter plays a rosewood square piano, and the rest of the family, dressed in Sunday best, gathers around under the mother's gaze. Though the father is there, he pays more attention to his newspaper than to his daughter's music. Women's place was in the home, and men's was in the larger world.

Courtesy of Frederick R. Selch, SI photograph by Rob Harrell.

This 1875 lithograph by Parsloe and Vance of New York captures the sometimes one-sided nature of the pleasures derived when a mature woman continued to sit down at the piano.

Courtesy of Peters Print Collection, National Museum of American History, SI.

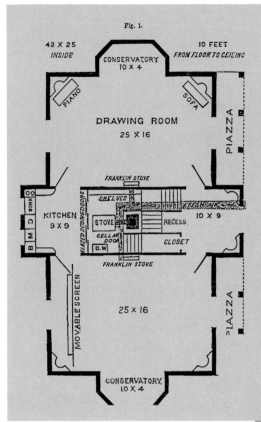

In 1869, Harriet Beecher Stowe, author of *Uncle Tom's Cabin,* and her sister Catherine E. Beecher, published a book on home management. This floor plan shows the placement of the required piano in the "drawing room." Of course, the piano was located centrally—where the TV would be today.

Reproduction from *The American Woman's Home, or, Principles of Domestic Science: Being a Guide to the Formation and Maintenance of Economical, Healthful, Beautiful and Christian Homes* (1869), courtesy of Harriet Beecher Stowe Center, Hartford, Connecticut.

A dutiful mother brings music into the lives of her children by singing with them at the piano in this 1863 lithograph, *Star-Spangled Banner,* by Thomas Sinclair of Philadelphia.

Courtesy of Peters Print Collection, National Museum of American History, Smithsonian Institution, SI photograph.

AMERICANS TAKE THE LEAD

Much of the piano industry through the middle of the 1800s was carried on in craft shops, where a few workers used hand tools to build small numbers of pianos. Though some makers such as John Broadwood & Sons in London and Erard in Paris had larger factories in the earlier part of the century, full assembly-line production had some years to wait. As the century went on, new factory methods appeared in both Europe and America, spawned by the Industrial Revolution and innovations in technologies of transportation and communication.

In Boston, Chickering & Sons, the leading U.S. maker, began a new factory in 1853. When completed, it was second only to the national Capitol in size. Increasingly steam engines powered machinery, and some companies specialized in making component parts for manufacturers and technicians. The day when a single worker could make a piano from start to finish was over. Workers had specialized tasks, and some critics thought that efficiency had triumphed over art. But the best of the factory-made pianos were excellent, and several famous companies of the period are still with us: the names of Bechstein, Blüthner, Steinway & Sons, and Schimmel stand alongside companies with earlier starts such as Bösendorfer, Petrof, and Erard.

Late nineteenth-century pianos contained most of the essentials of the modern instrument. Their increased volume, brilliance of tone, and greater stability in tuning was the result of the general adoption of iron frames. The range grew to the modern standard of 88 keys, and instruments began to take on standard sizes, approximately 9 feet long for concert grand pianos, about 5 feet high for standard uprights, and smaller sizes of both grands and uprights.

By the 1880s, almost all makers had adopted Erard's "repetition" action, and standard action designs for uprights became increasingly common. New inventions such as cross-stringing, in which longer bass strings cross above shorter tenor strings, permitted enriched tone and power to match the textures of later Romantic music and the increasing demands of twentieth-century musical styles, such as those of Claude Debussy, Sergei Prokofiev, and Béla Bartók.

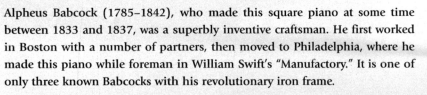

Alpheus Babcock (1785–1842), who made this square piano at some time between 1833 and 1837, was a superbly inventive craftsman. He first worked in Boston with a number of partners, then moved to Philadelphia, where he made this piano while foreman in William Swift's "Manufactory." It is one of only three known Babcocks with his revolutionary iron frame.

SI photograph by Robert Lautman.

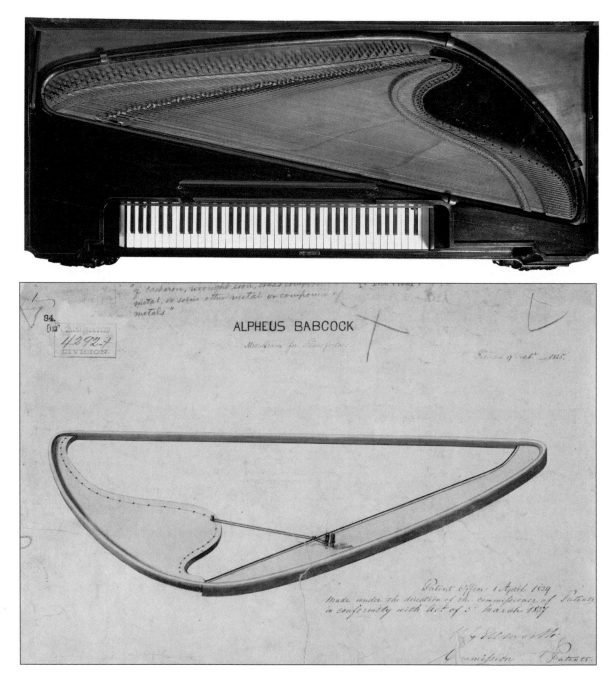

This view of Babcock's piano shows the most important American contribution to the piano's design—a single-piece cast-iron frame, patented in 1825. This invention allowed pianos to be larger, because the strings could be longer and stretched more tightly. The frame also resisted changes in humidity. Dampness causes wood to swell, raising the strings' tension and pitch, and dryness causes shrinkage, lowering tension and pitch. The modern piano, with its big, powerful sound, could not exist without Babcock's invention.

SI photograph by Robert Lautman; patent drawing from U.S. Patent Office.

Jonas Chickering (1797–1853) made several improvements to the piano's design. After Babcock returned to Boston to work for him in 1837, Chickering began to develop one-piece metal frames like this one for the grand piano, for which the company received a patent in 1843. Such patents helped Chickering become the first American manufacturer to build grands in quantity.

Patent drawing from U. S. Patent Office.

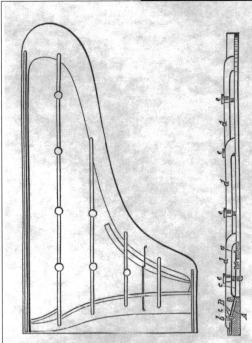

JONAS CHICKERING'S FULL SOLID-CAST GRAND METAL PLATE.

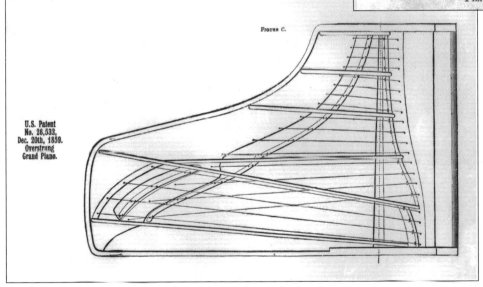

U.S. Patent
No. 26,532,
Dec. 20th, 1859.
Overstrung
Grand Piano.

FIGURE C.

Henry Steinway, Jr. (1830–1865) designed overstringing (or cross-stringing) for grand pianos that is still in use today. Setting the longer bass strings at an angle above the middle strings produced a richer tone, appropriate to the later Romantic music, and a more efficient amplification of sound by the soundboard. Steinway received this patent in 1859. Founded in 1853, Steinway & Sons soon offered Chickering stiff competition.

Patent drawing from U. S. Patent Office.

Jonas Chickering (1797–1853) and Heinrich Engelhard Steinweg (1797– 1871), later known as Henry Steinway, Sr., founders of rival companies, never met each other. Chickering, a New England Yankee, was a first-rate craftsman who made improvements to his piano designs at his workbench even as he became an astute and wealthy manufacturer. He died suddenly in 1853, and this memorial bust (left) evokes the same qualities as a eulogy describing Chickering as a "grand, square, and upright" person. Steinway and his family had built pianos in Germany before coming to New York in 1850. Steinway & Sons was established in 1853, and the family name was Americanized.

Chickering bust by Thomas Ball (Boston, 1854) courtesy of M. Steinert & Sons, Boston; Steinway bust by J. Graef (New York , 1871) courtesy of Steinway & Sons; SI photographs by Robert Harrell.

Only two years after this beautiful grand piano was built by Chickering & Sons (Boston, 1865), the firm won a gold medal at the World Exposition in Paris for a nearly identical piano. The American virtuoso Gottschalk used Chickering grands like this in his American tours.

SI photograph.

Upon Jonas Chickering's death his sons, from left to right, Thomas E. (1824–1871), Charles Francis or Frank (1827–1891), and George (1830–1899) took on their father's flourishing business. Thomas gave technical and commercial leadership as president. Frank combined the talents of inventor and promoter. George oversaw the factory operations in Boston. However, Chickering's fortunes declined with this second generation, and family ownership ended in the 1890s.

SI photographs.

This fully modern Steinway & Sons grand piano, made in New York in 1892, has all of Steinway's late 1800s' innovations: modern action, cross-stringing, and the middle "sostenuto" pedal (with which the player can sustain selected notes or chords). The piano was used by Ignacy Jan Paderewski for his first American tour, which cemented his reputation as a concert superstar. He proudly signed the frame, "This piano has been played by me in 75 concerts during 1892 and 1893."

SI photograph.

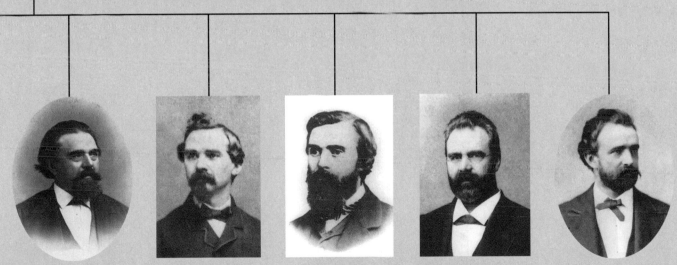

Five of Heinrich Steinweg's sons, from left to right, C. F. Theodore (1825–1889) Charles G. (1829–1865), Henry, Jr. (1830–1865), William (1835–1896), and Albert Steinway (1840–1877), furthered the firm's prominence. Henry, Jr., obtained several patents and Charles oversaw the factory operations. A genius in design, Theodore received 41 patents and perfected the upright for American homes. Albert supervised the factory after Charles's death. William added marketing and financial talent to the mix. His innovations were copied by other manufacturers: sponsoring tours by famous pianists, shrewd advertising, and building a company town that provided workers with housing, schools, and church. Steinway daughters, on the other hand, participated only through their husbands and sons. Four generations of a large, talented family helped Steinway & Sons to excel and prosper well into the 20th century.

Courtesy of Henry Z. Steinway, SI photographs.

This 1873 advertising "show card" printed by Major & Knapp of New York featured all aspects of Steinway & Sons operations. Steinway sent the card to its dealers all over the country for display in their showrooms.

Courtesy of Steinway & Sons; SI photograph by Robert Harrell.

CHICKERING & SONS'
PIANO-FORTE MANUFACTORY.
Tremont Street, BOSTON.

Chickering's new factory, begun in 1853 in Boston's Back Bay, was hailed as "the largest building in the United States excepting only the national Capitol." A shining new steam engine powered sawing and planing machines and an elevator big enough to hold "a comfortable dinner party." Workers there made or assembled the same parts repeatedly year after year. The building now houses artists' lofts and apartments.

Lithograph by J. H. Buford, Boston, courtesy of M. Steinert & Sons, Boston, SI photograph by Robert Harrell.

The addition of the steam engine brought not only power for manufacturing but also admiration from visitors to Chickering's Boston factory, as seen in this illustration from *Scientific American*, October 28, 1878.

Courtesy of Smithsonian Institution Libraries, SI photograph.

Piano manufacturers actively promoted concert life throughout the United States, and Steinway built a hall in New York. Chickering built halls there and in Boston. The noted pianist Hans von Bülow played at the 1875 inauguration of Chickering Hall in New York, pictured here, as part of an American tour under Chickering sponsorship. William Steinway, attending the opening, declared the hall a success.

From *Music Trade Review*, New York, 1875, courtesy of John R. Anderson.

In 1919 Steinway & Sons launched an inspired advertising campaign featuring big-name pianists such as Paderewski playing "The Instrument of the Immortals." The approach ever after associated Steinway pianos with the excellence of great artists in the public's mind and linked the company's name to themes of art, music, and achievement.

Advertisement by N. W. Ayar, Philadelphia, 1920s, Archives of the National Museum of American History, SI.

Albert Weber became Steinway's principal competitor in the 1870s, just as the Chickering company began to falter. Weber made few technical innovations. He simply made extremely fine pianos like this 1876 upright and sold them at fair prices. Beautifully decorated by Herter Brothers of New York, this instrument helped Weber challenge Steinway at the Philadelphia Centennial Exhibition in 1876. And it illustrated the rising popularity of the upright over the square.

SI photograph by Robert Lautman.

The nieces of Library of Congress worker Jewel Mazique practice their piano lesson.

Photograph by John Collier (Washington, D.C., 1942), U.S. Office of War Information Collection, courtesy of the Library of Congress.

John Thompson's *Teaching Little Fingers to Play*, whether published in 1936, like this copy, or printed yesterday, remains the familiar "little red book" of first lessons for generations of students.

Courtesy of DeVincent Collection of Illustrated American Sheet Music, Archives Center, National Museum of American History, SI photograph by John Tsantes.

TAKING PIANO

Piano playing and piano teaching became significant as an acceptable means for women to earn a living in a day when marriage was assumed to be the goal of female life. As the most accomplished and respected musician in town, the American piano teacher—nearly always a woman—often led the charge to raise and broaden standards of education. Even though the number of successful women professional pianists expanded in the twentieth century, most performed relatively rarely while teaching many students.

Taking piano lessons has been a rite of passage for generations of children. Where earlier generations saw piano playing as a social grace that was morally uplifting, modern studies suggest that the hand and brain skills required in piano playing are actually beneficial to cognitive development.

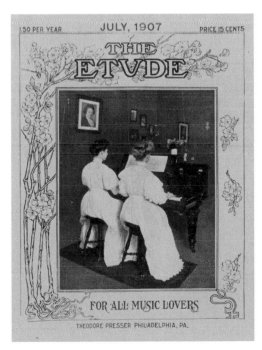

If you've studied piano, you're probably one of the millions who've had a few lessons from Carl Czerny (1791–1857). The composer of thousands of "études" ("studies" or piano exercises) still used today, this Vienna-based pianist and teacher was a pupil of Beethoven. Czerny in turn taught Franz Liszt and some of the most influential piano teachers of the nineteenth century.

Lithograph by Josef Kriehuber (Vienna, 1833), courtesy of Royal College of Music, London.

Between 1883 and 1957, music teachers and students pored over *The Etude*, published monthly by Theodore Presser in Philadelphia, for the latest articles on teaching and music appreciation.

From *The Etude* (July 1907), courtesy of Smithsonian Institution Libraries.

Louisiana-born Amy Fay (1844–1928), seen here in 1875, was one of many promising young American musicians who went to Europe in the 1800s to finish their training. Fay described her studies with Franz Liszt and other noted teachers in a sparkling book, *Music-Study in Germany,* and toured the United States offering "lecture-recitals" that combined piano solos and commentary.

Courtesy of the Preston H. Tuttle Collection, Institute for Studies in Pragmatism, Texas Tech University.

In addition to teaching piano lessons, Henrietta Fuller Robinson (1904–1998) directed church choirs, organized concerts and recitals, and gave her energy to dozens of projects for cultural improvement in her southern New Jersey African American community.

Photograph (1920s) courtesy of Henrietta Booth Robinson Fuller Collection.

From the 1820s on, inventors devised mechanical aids to piano practice. The makers of the Technicon (circa 1885–1890) claimed that this "hand gymnasium" helped pianists by stretching the sinews between the fingers and strengthening the wrist and forearm. Unfortunately, most of these devices actually stiffened the player's soft tissues and occasionally caused permanent injury.

SI photograph.

PIANOS FOR ALL

By the late 1800s, pianos became widely available as manufacturing and distribution methods led to lower prices. Joseph P. Hale, a Yankee businessman, had the vision of a piano in every home in America. He assembled inexpensive instruments from parts bought from other companies to give music to people who could never afford to patronize the famous makers. Pianos could be purchased with modest monthly payments from the manufacturer or music store or through mail-order catalogs. Traveling salesmen sometimes carried them through rural America in specially modified Model T cars, and a family could touch and try a piano right in its own front yard!

The Great Depression of the 1930s dramatically slowed piano production; ordinary people simply could not afford instruments. Some very small new models were introduced, such as the "spinet," a little upright scarcely higher than the keyboard and correspondingly weak in tone. World War II practically brought piano manufacturing to a halt, when such companies as Steinway & Sons manufactured U. S. Army gliders and even coffins instead of pianos.

The Atwood piano loader, shown on the back of a Ford runabout somewhere in rural Iowa in the 1920s, allowed traveling piano salesmen to bring sample pianos to the very doorsteps of rural America. A slick salesman might bring a piano to a farmhouse and ask if he could leave it while he had his car repaired. With any luck, by the time he returned a few days later, the family would have decided it couldn't live without the piano.

Courtesy of Warshaw Collection of Business Americana, Archives Center, National Museum of American History, SI.

"Hail to the Chief!"

"A good instrument at a cheap rate" was the watchword of Joseph P. Hale (1819–1883). His success at assembling pianos from ready-made parts and building a market in the American West meant that more American homes boasted pianos than ever before. But his habit of producing low-cost pianos, sometimes labeled with names that echoed established brands (such as "Stanley & Sons"), led to attacks from his more conservative competitors, as seen in this 1876 cartoon. Nonetheless, Hale prospered and revolutionized the piano industry.

From *Music Trade Review,* 1876 and 1879, courtesy of John R. Anderson.

Alfred Dolge (1842–1922), pictured in the 1880s, was a key supplier of the mass-produced parts that led to more affordable American pianos. A German immigrant, Dolge established a large factory in 1874 to make piano felts and soundboards in Brockett's Bridge, New York (renamed Dolgeville in 1881). He won high marks from organized labor for providing workers with generous pensions and for furnishing his model community with schools and a clubhouse equipped with a stage and gymnasium.

Courtesy of the Dolgeville-Manheim Historical Society Museum.

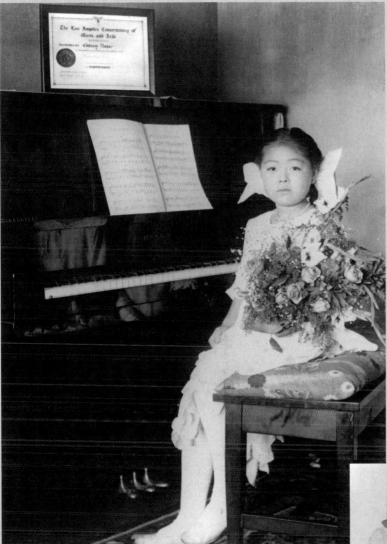

Thanks to the success of efforts to bring pianos to nearly everyone, by the 20th century the vast array of Americans enjoying its pleasures included young Marjorie Yamamoto of Los Angeles, right, displaying her recital awards in the 1930s, and a group of dudes, above, harmonizing in the back room of a beer parlor in Birney, Montana, in 1939.

Yamamoto photograph courtesy of the Japanese American National Museum; "dudes" by Arthur Rothstein, Farm Security Administration/Office of War Information Collection, courtesy of the Library of Congress.

If you lived far from stores and beyond the reach of traveling salesmen, you could still order a piano by mail. The 1902 Sears, Roebuck catalog offered an upright at $98.50, about one-fifth of a year's wages for the average workman in 1900.

Courtesy of Smithsonian Institution Libraries.

The Console-Spinet made by Sohmer & Company in Long Island City, New York, was one of a dozen featured in the *Piano Trade Magazine* article, "Piano Fashions of 1937." To encourage purchases of these small instruments (the Sohmer is 3 feet 3 inches high), manufacturers emphasized furniture design over sound quality.

From *Piano Trade Magazine,* January 1937, courtesy of Smithsonian Institution Libraries.

MUSIC TRADES

By 1900, pianos, sheet music, and other instruments were widely available at music stores in big cities and small towns across the United States. As the chief source of home musical entertainment, pianos were in demand. Sales of sheet music flourished, and a piano technician's trade had developed to keep pianos in tune and in good condition.

One of the services offered by Ludwig Music House of St. Louis, Missouri, in about 1905, was a pianist to demonstrate sheet music, above. At left, phonographs were crowding out the pianos in an upstate New York music shop by 1920.

Photos courtesy of Robert McDowell, Corbis Bettmann/UPI.

Newspaper readers sometimes received music supplements like this one of the popular song "Annie Laurie," sponsored by the Bromo-Seltzer Company of Baltimore in the late 1890s. Because piano owners tended to hold on to these pages, businesses found that they were a good place to advertise.

National Museum of American History, Smithsonian Institution. SI photograph.

The Oliver Ditson company of Boston was established in 1835 as a small publishing firm that also sold musical instruments. By 1890 it was the largest music publisher in the United States.

From *Dwight's Journal of Music,* July 21, 1860, courtesy of Smithsonian Institution Libraries.

A technician adjusts a cabinet piano at John Broadwood & Sons of London in 1842. Herman Krausser, above right, tunes one of the 33 pianos at NBC Radio City Studios in New York, 1942. The wrench he uses to turn the tuning pins is called a tuning hammer.

From *Days at the Factories* by George Dodd (London, 1843), and *Piano Trade Magazine* (April 1942), courtesy of Smithsonian Institution Libraries.

Advertisements such as this one from the November 1903 issue of *The Etude* encouraged women and blind people to learn piano tuning. The "Tune-a-phone" was something like a mouth organ. The tuner generated the pitch by blowing through a long tube.

Courtesy of Smithsonian Institution Libraries.

The TUNE-A-PHONE in Operation

LEARN PIANO TUNING

HERE'S A RICH FIELD
Be Independent and Your Own Employer

This old and dignified profession is positively being successfully taught by mail by a new scientific method. We are the inventors and control the TUNE-A-PHONE—the scientific invention that teaches you in your own home.

The course includes tuning, action regulating, repairing, etc., is thorough and easy to understand, with attention from Prof. Bryant to each student. After you have graduated and received your diploma we help you start in business.

Here's a real opportunity.

Every musician should have knowledge of piano tuning, regulating, etc. We give free a TUNE-A-PHONE (an invaluable assistant) to each student.

Note the simplicity, adaptability, and compactness of the instrument. It answers at once as a tuning-fork and a third hand, and is so small it can be carried in the pocket. The only instrument of its kind ever invented.

Write to-day and let us send you complete information, testimonials, endorsements from piano manufacturers, etc., of our School.

NILES BRYANT SCHOOL OF PIANO TUNING
200 Music Hall, Battle Creek, Mich.

THE AFRICAN AMERICAN LEGACY

s affordable pianos became part of many African American communities, new musical styles emerged. From the distinctive rhythms and forms of African American religious and social music grew new kinds of dance music, leading to ragtime as first popularized by the phenomenal Scott Joplin. Spreading across musical America and to Europe, ragtime gave birth to jazz, which became a pervasive musical influence during the twentieth century. Pianists and pianos lived at the center of jazz, as names like "Jelly Roll" Morton, Duke Ellington, Dave Brubeck, Eubie Blake, George Shearing, Art Tatum, Mary Lou Williams, and many more attest.

Born in the African American community sometime after the Civil War, ragtime brought a syncopated, or "ragged," beat to marches, classical music, folk songs and dance tunes. Ragtime's syncopation was derived from the infectious rhythm behind the strutting cakewalk, above, an international dance craze of around 1900.

Cakewalk No. 1 (1890s) courtesy of American Ragtime Company.

African Jazz No. 5, 1990, quilt by Michael A. Cummings.
Lent by the artist.

With the piano's support, African American churches developed distinctive gospel styles. Blind pianist Arizona Dranes (1905–1960) above left, created an energetic piano-rag style to accompany the singing, shouting and holy dancing in Pentecostal and Holiness churches.

Courtesy of Church of God in Christ Archives.

Scott Joplin (1868–1917), above right, gave elegance and polish to the music of black dance halls, creating classical ragtime. His immensely popular *Maple Leaf Rag* (1899) became the model for classical ragtime compositions. Joplin photograph, courtesy of Special Collections, Fisk University Library; DeVincent Collection of Illustrated Sheet Music, Archives Center, National Museum of American History, SI.

James Hubert "Eubie" Blake (1883–1983), pictured here circa 1910s, popularized the fast, volatile East Coast Rag style. *The Charleston Rag* (1899), his teen-age "fingerbuster," helped to create some early forms of jazz.

Courtesy of Eubie Blake National Jazz Institute and Cultural Center.

Ferdinand Joseph "Jelly Roll" Morton (1885–1941) liked to call himself "the inventor of jazz." Whether or not the claim is accepted, this New Orleans pianist mixed blues styles and improvisation into the ragtime rhythm, and used the piano like a band, imitating trombone effects with one hand and clarinets with the other.

Photograph, 1920, courtesy of Duncan P. Scheidt Collection, Institute of Jazz Studies, Rutgers University.

Called "the First Lady of Jazz Piano," Mary Lou Williams (1910–1981) was one of the most influential performers and arrangers of her time. Besides short works for the piano, she composed larger orchestral pieces, such as *Zodiac Suite* (1946).

Photograph, 1946, by James Kriegsman, courtesy of Institute of Jazz Studies, Rutgers University.

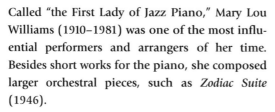

James P. Johnson (1891–1955) was the father of stride piano, named for the long, muscular "strides" taken by the left hand. Classically trained, Johnson (seen here around 1940) was a powerful, athletic player whose style influenced many jazz greats.

Photograph courtesy of Smithsonian Folkways Archives.

Edward Kennedy "Duke" Ellington (1899–1974) was more than a jazz pianist. He was one of the 20th century's great composers. Born in Washington, D.C., he created more than 2,000 works, many of them for piano and orchestra, and led his own legendary orchestra for more than 50 years. On this Steinway grand piano (New York, 1960), which once stood in Ellington's New York apartment, he composed the music for his *Sacred Concerts* (1965–1973).

Portrait bust, 1988, by Ed Dwight, courtesy of Marilyn and Calvin Gross, SI photograph by Dane Penland. Piano courtesy of the Cathedral of St. John the Divine, New York, SI photograph by Richard Strauss.

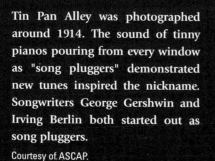

JEROME H. REMICK & COMPANY.

MUSIC PUB

45 WHITNEY WARNER
DETROIT MUSIC NEW YORK

WHITNEY WARNE
MUSIC

PRINTER

PPER

MUSIC PUBLISHERS.

LIPPER.

NEW YORK CLIPPER

JEROME H. REMICK & COMPANY

45 MUSIC PUBLISHERS

EMICK & COMPANY.
NER PUBLISHING CO

WILLIAM
MORRIS

THOMAS YOUNG

Tin Pan Alley was photographed around 1914. The sound of tinny pianos pouring from every window as "song pluggers" demonstrated new tunes inspired the nickname. Songwriters George Gershwin and Irving Berlin both started out as song pluggers.

Courtesy of ASCAP.

TIN PAN ALLEY

ew York's Tin Pan Alley was the heart of popular music publishing in the early 1900s. There men or women of either stupendous talent or no ability whatsoever (or something in between) vied for the chance to have their songs published and promoted by popular singers of the day. Topics included everything from love and despair to religion, patriotism, and current events. Widely produced in cheap but colorful editions, Tin Pan Alley music was sold in music stores, department stores, and five-and-dimes around the world. The piano was the beginning, the middle, and the end of the process.

This upright transposing piano was made in 1940 by Weser Brothers, New York, for Irving Berlin (1888-1989). Like many Tin Pan Alley pianists, Berlin was self-taught, preferring to play on the black keys ("The key of C," he once said, "is for people who study music"). The transposing mechanism shifted the keyboard to allow him to stay on the black keys but produce music in other keys.

SI photograph.

Renowned caricaturist Al Hirschfeld created a pantheon of popular song composers and lyricists in 1983. At the keyboard: Duke Ellington, George Gershwin, and Hoagy Carmichael. Around them (left to right): Richard Rodgers, Lorenz Hart, Cole Porter, Harold Arlen, Dorothy Fields, Jerome Kern, Johnny Mercer, Ira Gershwin, and Irving Berlin.

Pen-and-ink drawing by Al Hirschfeld courtesy of National Portrait Gallery, Smithsonian Institution, and Margo Feiden Galleries.

PIANOS WITHOUT PIANISTS

he tremendous growth of "player pianos" from early in the twentieth century brought piano music into homes even where no one played. Player pianos offered renditions of popular tunes, hymns, jazz, Tin Pan Alley, and Broadway show songs suitable for family singalongs. More advanced models were able to reproduce performances by important pianists. Production of player pianos outpaced other pianos during the early 1920s, but fell off with the Great Depression. As radios, phonographs, and movies captured the public imagination by the mid-1920s, the player pianos kept pianos from succumbing entirely to the new competition, and recordings kept the piano in the public ear. Piano playing by actual people regained popularity after World War II, and it wasn't until the end of the century that new, electronic forms of reproducing pianos again captured the public's imagination.

Player pianos like this one required a "performer" to work the tempo, volume, and expression controls and to pump the pedals that made the machine work. But even a little child could do it, as seen in this farmhouse near Cedarville, N. J., in 1940.

Photograph by Jack Delano, Farm Security Administration Collection, courtesy of Library of Congress.

This player piano, made by Gabler & Bros., New York (circa 1925), promised fun almost without skill or effort. It is a normal piano, playable like any other, but the player pedals fold down, and controls operate a perforated paper roll for an automatic player. By 1923 nearly 60 percent of the 347,000 pianos produced in America were players.

SI photograph by Robert Lautman.

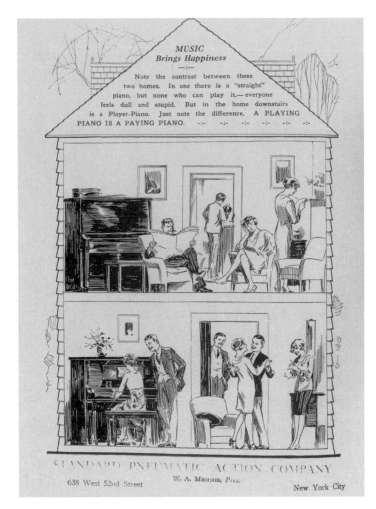

Advertising for player pianos emphasized the skill needed to play normal pianos. Here the bored family sitting near the silent instrument contrasts with the lively party downstairs, energized by the player piano.

Advertisement for Standard Pneumatic Action Company (1920), courtesy of Harvey Roehl.

Ignacy Jan Paderewski warranted that this paper roll, developed for use in a "reproducing" piano, recreated his actual performance. Some pneumatic player piano rolls had printed song lyrics along the edge for singers to follow. Early rolls required a player to work controls for tempo, loudness, and accents. Later rolls, like the one seen here, were able to control these dynamics.

Duo-Art roll, Division of Cultural History collections, NMAH, SI photograph by Richard Strauss.

At the end of the 20th century, player pianos entered the electronic age. Yamaha's Disklavier uses not paper rolls but CDs to reproduce performances. And the home pianist can record to the CD, play it back, and even correct the wrong notes!

SI photograph by Richard Strauss.

When the piano was first introduced into Japan, its discipline and art resonated with Japanese culture. The Japanese soon began manufacturing pianos for national consumption, though this painting by Daizaburo Nakamura (1926) depicts a woman in traditional kimono playing a Czech piano. Japan, Korea, and China are now the world leaders in piano manufacture.

Courtesy of Kyoto Municipal Museum of Art.

THE ASIAN EXPERIENCE

fter World War II, manufacturing leadership shifted from the United States to Asia. By 1970 Japan was the scene of the largest production, and Yamaha had become the world's largest manufacturer. In the 1980s and later, Korea became a very important source for pianos (Young Chang is its largest maker), and during the 1990s, China widely expanded its piano industry to serve an enormous market. A number of American and European companies faded away or were absorbed into others. In 2001, the Baldwin Company in Cincinnati, Ohio, made Wurlitzer and Chickering pianos, and famous old brands are now made by Korean makers Samick and Young Chang.

A Japanese delegation in 1871 observed American school children singing to piano accompaniment and praised the instrument for "stimulating the mind and cultivating the disposition." Nagai Shigeko, a young member of the delegation, remained in the United States to study at Vassar College. Returning home, she became one of Japan's first piano teachers.

Courtesy of Vassar College Libraries.

Torakusu Yamaha (1851–1916) largely began Japan's piano industry. Originally a medical technician, his imagination was fired by an invitation to repair a reed organ in 1887. Two years later he opened an organ factory. His Nippon Gakki Company made its first upright piano in 1900, its first grand in 1902, and won a prize for grand pianos at the St. Louis World Exposition in 1904.

Photograph courtesy of Yamaha Corporation of America.

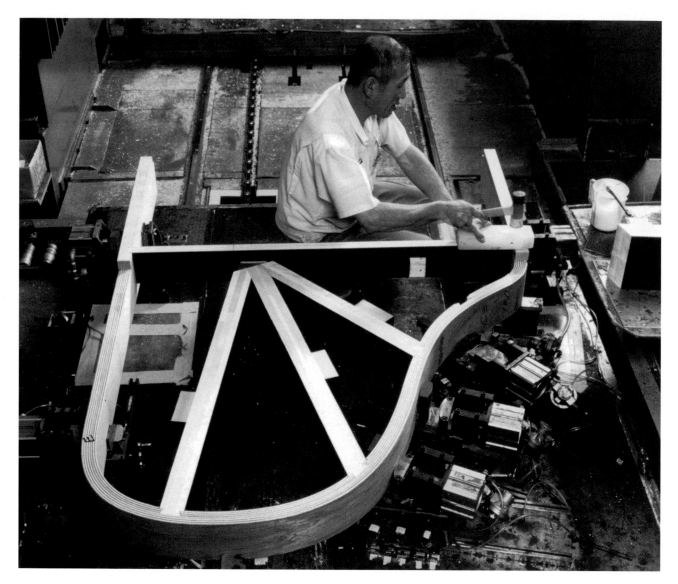

Early Yamahas were luxury items: a grand piano cost as much as a house in Japan, an upright half of that. Assembly-line techniques and robotic machinery, shown here about 1990, have aided handwork to streamline the process and lower costs, and production has boomed.

Courtesy of Yamaha Corporation of America.

Today more pianos are made and played in East Asia than anywhere else. This "Pro 2000" is the latest design from Yamaha of Hamamatsu, Japan, the world's largest piano manufacturer. A normal piano, it can also be a player piano, record and play back what is played on it, play a commercial CD or video, download from the Internet, and display the score of a work on a TV monitor.

Courtesy of Yamaha.

A digital piano like this Roland HP-335 has built-in speakers and headphone jacks but produces sound electronically. Some models add instrumental sounds and MIDI (Musical Instrument Digital Interface), giving more scope for learning and composing. Ikutaro Kakehashi, the founder of Japan's Roland Corporation, was the guiding spirit behind the cooperative development of MIDI, the software by which all electronic instruments can communicate with and control each other.

Courtesy of Roland Corporation U.S.

ELECTRIFYING

W hile music had been made electronically in the late nineteenth century, it wasn't until after World War II that musicians became taken with electric and electronic keyboards. These instruments are programmed to make many different instrumental sounds. Headphones make possible complete silence while playing, and amplification allows greater loudness in concerts than mere human muscles can produce. Computers and MIDI (Musical Instrument Digital Interface) software ease the use of keyboards for composing and the simultaneous control of several instruments in concert.

Early synthesized piano sound was unsatisfactory. More recently, electronic keyboard makers have used "sampling" for piano sound. A computer program samples a digitally recorded piano sound many times a second to produce a somewhat simplified sound, but recognizably that of a piano. The electronic keyboard, therefore, can make no piano sound unless someone first played on a "real" piano.

Technically speaking, because they have no hammers or strings, electronic keyboards and digital pianos are not true pianos. Their keys activate sounds digitally programmed on microchips, and piano sounds are one among a great many available instrumental sounds.

Still, pianos continue to be made, and sometimes people even decide to "upgrade" from their electronic keyboards to pianos.

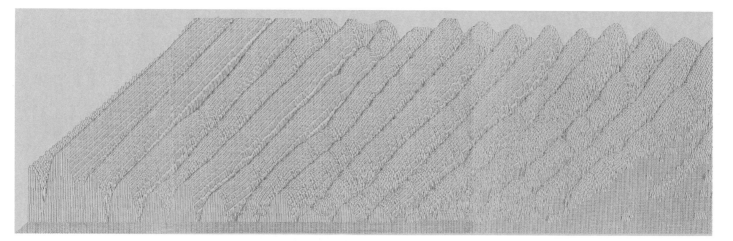

This graphic represents part of the sampled sound of a single piano note.
Courtesy of Roland Corporation U.S.

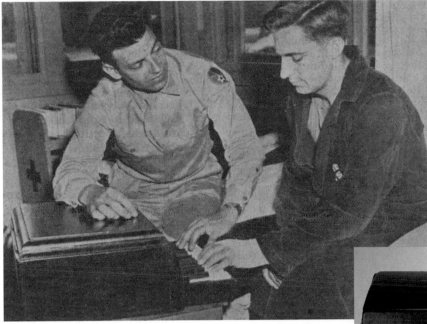

Harold Rhodes (1910–2000) experimented early with electric pianos and manufactured them beginning in the late 1950s with guitar builder Leo Fender (1909–1991). During World War II, Rhodes used parts from wrecked airplanes to design a piano for wounded airmen in hospitals, above. With 29 notes, it was small enough to play in bed, and had a light, bell-like sound. The Fender-Rhodes Mark I Stage Piano (1971–1973), right, has hammers that strike metal rods, whose vibrations are amplified electrically.

Photograph of Rhodes and Air Corps piano (1944) courtesy of *Newsweek;* SI photograph of Fender-Rhodes Mark I by Richard Strauss.

From top, Yamaha's DX-7 (1987) was an innovative keyboard synthesizer, and Korg's Triton (1999) and Roland's XP-80 (1999) produce "sampled" sounds. Keyboards are often attached via MIDI (Musical Instrument Digital Interface) to computers. Japanese companies have led the development of electronic keyboards.

SI photograph by Richard Strauss; rack, gift of Ultimate Support Systems, Inc.

MASS AUDIENCES

Thanks to the mass media, the piano has reached every corner of the world and its most famous artists are universally recognized. The resulting cultural interchange crosses national and geographical boundaries: Japanese pianists play jazz, African ones perform classical European music, and North American players master Latino styles. The Chinese music scene includes lively piano production and performance.

We leave predictions about the future to seers and prophets. But as the favorite entry point into music making for children everywhere, the composer's mainstay, and the continuing centerpiece of the cultured home, the piano claims an assured standing in musical affections the world over.

The concert pictured here, a celebration of the return of Hong Kong to China in 1997, featured 97 Guangzhou Pearl River grand pianos played simultaneously.

Courtesy of Guangzhou Piano Manufacturers, Guangzhou, China.

This packed salesroom floor at Jordan-Kitt's Music store in Sterling, Virginia, attests to the continuing popularity of the piano in the 21st century.

Courtesy of Jordan-Kitt's Music.

When television dominated American leisure time in the 1950s, Liberace (Wladziu Valentino, 1919–1987) mastered the medium with lavish costumes, candelabra, and his flamboyant manner. To harmonize with Liberace's glittering image—involving some nostalgia, perhaps, for the opulence of the Medici court of 1700—the Baldwin Company customized this fine grand with 125 pounds of clear Austrian rhinestones.

Photo of Liberace performance in the 1980s courtesy of Liberace Foundation and Museum, Las Vegas, Nevada.

Billy Joel (1949-) performs in *Piano Grand! A Smithsonian Celebration,* filmed for PBS in March 2000.

SI photograph by Hugh Talman.

Opposite: Detail from Chickering square piano, Boston, 1850.

SI photograph by Robert Lautman.

INSTRUMENTS DISPLAYED IN *PIANO 300*

Pianos are arranged in chronological order.

See pages 11, 13.

GRAND PIANO, BARTOLOMEO CRISTOFORI, FLORENCE 1722
Lent by Museo Nazionale degli Strumenti Musicali, Rome

49 keys (4 octaves)

Action:	Cristofori action
Strings:	brass, 2 strings for each note
Hammers:	deerskin pads on wood blocks
Hand-operated stop:	keyboard shift (una corda, hammers strike one string)
Soundboard:	cypress
Frame:	wood
Case:	poplar

This is the second-oldest piano in existence, one of three known by Cristofori, the inventor of the piano. It was returned to Rome on Feb. 21, 2001.

GRAND PIANO, DAVID SUTHERLAND and KEITH HILL, ANN ARBOR, MI, and MANCHESTER, NH, 1995–98
Copy of Bartolomeo Cristofori piano, University Musikinstrumentenmuseum, Leipzig, Germany, 1726
Lent by The Schubert Club Museum of Musical Instruments, St. Paul, Minnesota

49 keys (4 octaves)

Action:	Cristofori action
Strings:	brass, 2 strings for each note
Hammers:	deerskin pads on rolled parchment
Hand-operated stop:	keyboard shift (una corda: hammers strike one string)
Soundboard:	cypress
Frame:	wood
Case:	American poplar

This instrument substituted for the 1722 Cristofori from February through October 2001.

See page 14.

SQUARE PIANO, JOHANNES ZUMPE and BUNTEBART, LONDON, 1770
National Museum of American History, Smithsonian Institution, catalog no. 60.1390

60 keys (5 octaves—no FF#)

Action:	Zumpe single action
Strings:	brass and iron, 2 strings for each note
Hammers:	bookbinder's leather on wood core
Hand-operated levers (left to right):	
	1. upper damper lifter (allows strings to keep vibrating)
	2. lower damper lifter
	3. harp stop (moves cloth against strings to shorten tone)
Frame:	wood
Case:	mahogany veneer; stained beech reproduction stand

See page 16.

GRAND PIANO, JEAN-LOUIS DULCKEN, MUNICH, ca. 1788
National Museum of American History, Smithsonian Institution, gift of Hugo Worch, catalog no. 303,537

63 keys (5 octaves + 2 keys)

Action:	"Viennese" action
Strings:	brass and iron, 2 strings for each note
Hammers:	deerskin on wood core
Knee levers:	damper lifter (allows strings to keep vibrating)
Frame:	wood
Case:	cherry veneer

SQUARE PIANO, CHARLES ALBRECHT, PHILADELPHIA, 1792–1795
National Museum of American History, Smithsonian Institution, gift of Hugo Worch, catalog no. 288,398

61 keys (5 octaves)

Action:	Viennese action
Strings:	brass wound and plain brass, iron, 2 strings for each note
Hammers:	deerskin on wood core
Knee levers (left to right):	1. moderator (moves cloth between hammers and strings)
	2. damper lifter (allows strings to keep vibrating)
	3. swell (opens wooden shutters at right for louder sound)
Frame:	wood
Case:	mahogany veneer

See page 17.

GRAND PIANO, JOHN BROADWOOD & SONS, LONDON, serial no. 715A, 1794
National Museum of American History, Smithsonian Institution, gift of Hugo Worch, catalog no. 303,530

68 keys (5 2/3 octaves)

Action:	English grand action
Strings:	brass and iron, 3 strings for each note
Hammers:	leather on wood core
Pedals (left to right):	1. una corda (moves action so hammers strike one string)
	2. damper lifter (allows strings to keep vibrating)
Frame:	wood, iron gap spacers
Case:	mahogany veneer

See page 27.

PORTABLE UPRIGHT PIANO, JOHN ISAAC HAWKINS, PHILADELPHIA, serial no. 6, 1801
National Museum of American History, Smithsonian Institution, gift of Hugo Worch, catalog no. 313,619

61 keys (5 octaves)

Action:	Hawkins upright action
Strings:	iron, 2 strings for each note
Hammers:	layers of felt (originally leather)
Pedals (left to right):	1. moderator (moves felt between hammers and strings)
	2. swell (opens shutters below keyboard for louder sound)
Frame:	wood with iron bars behind soundboard
Case:	mahogany veneer with carrying handles

This very small instrument was patented by Hawkins, its inventor, as a "portable grand piano."

See page 28.

GIRAFFE PIANO, ANDRÉ STEIN, VIENNA, 1809–1811
National Museum of American History, Smithsonian Institution, gift of Hugo Worch, catalog no. 299,844

73 keys (6 octaves)

Action:	"Hanging" Viennese action
Strings:	brass and iron, 2 or 3 strings for each note
Hammers:	layers of leather on wood core
Pedals (left to right):	1. bassoon stop (moves a rod wrapped in parchment against vibrating string, to make a buzzing sound)
	2. damper lifter (allows strings to keep vibrating)
	3-4. moderator (moves cloth between hammers and strings to mute the sound)
	5. Janissary or Turkish music (drum and bell sounds)
	6. una corda (moves action so hammers strike one string)
Frame:	wood
Case:	mahogany veneer with silked front panels

See page 29.

SEWING-TABLE PIANO, UNKNOWN (GERMAN or AUSTRIAN), ca. 1820–1840
National Museum of American History, Smithsonian Institution, gift of Richard Piet, catalog no. 1992.0192.01

49 keys (4 octaves)

Action:	Viennese action
Strings:	iron, 1 or 2 strings for each note
Hammers:	white leather on wood core
Frame:	wood
Case:	rosewood veneer

See front cover, pages 33, 34.

SQUARE PIANO, ALPHEUS BABCOCK FOR WILLIAM SWIFT, PHILADELPHIA, serial no. 1517, 1833–1837
National Museum of American History, Smithsonian Institution, gift of Hugo Worch, catalog no. 315,690

73 keys (6 octaves)

Action:	Babcock patented articulated action
Strings:	iron, 2 strings for each note
Hammers:	felt-covered (probably originally deerskin)
Pedals (left to right):	1. moderator (moves leather between hammers and strings)
	2. damper lifter (allows strings to keep vibrating
Frame:	one-piece cast-iron frame (Babcock patent)
Case:	crotch mahogany veneer with inlays

See back cover, pages 26, 27, 73.

SQUARE PIANO, CHICKERING & SONS, BOSTON, serial no. 10683, 1850
National Museum of American History, Smithsonian Institution, gift of Richard P. Butrick, catalog no. 68.5

85 keys (7 octaves)
Action: Edwin Brown patented action
Strings: Copper wound and iron, 1 or 2 strings for each note
Hammers: layers of leather on wood core

Pedals (left to right):	1. moderator (moves felt between hammers and strings)
	2. damper lifter (allows strings to keep vibrating)
Frame:	one-piece iron frame, gilded and decorative
Case:	rosewood veneer

PIANO STOOL, UNKNOWN (AMERICAN), 1850s
National Museum of American History, Smithsonian Institution, gift of Mr. and Mrs. Franklin W. Wallin

MINIATURE GRAND PIANO, J. KIRKMAN & SON, LONDON, 1851
National Museum of American History, Smithsonian Institution, gift of Hugo Worch, catalog no. 315,751
80 keys (6 2/3 octaves)

Action:	English grand action
Strings:	copper wound and iron, 1 or 2 strings for each note
Hammers:	felt
Pedals (left to right):	1. una corda (hammer strikes only one string)
	2. damper lifter (allows strings to keep vibrating)
Soundboard:	spruce
Frame:	partial iron with tension bars, straight stringing
Case:	ebonized with gilt decoration

The piano was exhibited at the Crystal Palace exhibition, London, 1851; it has been claimed that it belonged to General Tom Thumb.

GRAND PIANO, ERARD, LONDON, serial no. 3964, 1854

National Museum of American History, Smithsonian Institution, gift of Dr. and Mrs. Herbert R. Axelrod and The Friends of Music at the Smithsonian, catalog no. 1991.0372.01

85 keys (7 octaves)

Action:	Erard repetition action of 1840
Strings:	copper-wound and plain steel, 1, 2, or 3 strings for each note
Hammers:	felt over leather on wood core
Pedals (left to right):	1. una corda (moves action so that hammers strike 1 less string)
	2. damper-lifter (allows strings to keep vibrating)
Frame:	partial iron frame with tension bars and spacers, straight-strung
Case:	rosewood veneer

See pages 6, 21.

The instrument was bought from Erard's London establishment by Queen Victoria in 1854 as a gift for Prince Albert. It was housed in Balmoral Castle, Scotland.

GRAND PIANO, CHICKERING & SONS, BOSTON, serial no. 27733, 1865

National Museum of American History, Smithsonian Institution, gift of Mrs. Henry Hoagland, catalog no. 1981.0625.01

88 keys (7 1/3 octaves)

Action:	Edwin Brown patented action
Strings:	copper-wound and plain steel, 1, 2, or 3 strings for each note
Hammers:	layers of felt
Pedals (left to right):	1. una corda (moves action to strike 2 of 3 strings)
	2. damper lifter (allow strings to keep vibrating)
Frame:	one-piece cast-iron frame, straight stringing
Case:	rosewood veneer

See page 36.

UPRIGHT PIANO, WEBER PIANO COMPANY, NEW YORK, serial no. 9957, 1876

National Museum of American History, Smithsonian Institution, catalog no. 1980.0360.01

88 keys (7 1/3 octaves)

Action:	tape-check upright action (probably not original)
Strings:	copper-wound and plain steel, 1, 2, or 3 strings for each note
Hammers:	felt
Pedals (left to right):	1. soft pedal (moves hammers closer to strings)
	2. damper lifter (allows strings to keep vibrating)
Frame:	double iron frame, one part in front of soundboard, one behind, bolted together, cross-stringing
Case:	ebonized with inlaid designs and gilded banding

See page 41.

This piano was designed by Herter Brothers, furniture designers, New York, and exhibited at the 1876 Philadelphia Centennial Exposition.

GRAND PIANO, STEINWAY & SONS, NEW YORK, serial no. 71227, 1892

National Museum of American History, Smithsonian Institution, gift of Steinway & Sons, catalog no. 74.7

88 keys (7 1/3 octaves)

Action:	repetition action
Strings:	copper-wound and plain steel, 1, 2, or 3 strings for each note
Hammers:	layers of felt
Pedals (left to right):	1. una corda (moves action to strike 2 of 3 strings)
	2. sostenuto (Steinway patent: lifts selected dampers)
	3. damper lifter (allows strings to keep vibrating)
Frame:	one-piece cast-iron, cross-stringing
Case:	French-polished black

See page 37.

This piano was played by Ignacy Jan Paderewski during his first U.S. tour, 1892-1893.

See page 62.

UPRIGHT PLAYER PIANO, GABLER & BROTHERS, NEW YORK, serial no. 158799, ca. 1925

National Museum of American History, Smithsonian Institution, catalog no. 71.12
88 keys (7 1/3 octaves)

Action:	tape-check upright action
Strings:	copper-wound and plain steel, 1, 2, or 3 strings for each note
Hammers:	felt
Pedals (left to right):	1. soft pedal (moves hammers closer to strings)
	2. dummy (does nothing)
	3. damper lifter (allows strings to keep vibrating)
Frame:	one-piece cast-iron upright frame, cross-stringing
Case:	mahogany veneer

Player mechanism by Standard Pneumatic Action Co.

See page 8.

GRAND PIANO, STEINWAY & SONS, MODEL D, NEW YORK, serial no. 295821, 1939

National Museum of American History, Smithsonian Institution, catalog no. 1989.0216.01

88 keys (7 1/3 octaves)

Action:	Steinway "accelerated" repetition action
Strings:	Copper-wound and plain steel, 1, 2, or 3 strings for each note
Hammers:	felt
Pedals (left to right):	1. una corda (moves hammers to strike 2 of 3 strings)
	2. sostenuto (Steinway patent, lifts selected dampers)
	3. damper lifter (allows strings to keep vibrating)
Frame:	one-piece cast-iron frame, cross-stringing
Case:	maple veneer with gilded decoration

The instrument was designed by Walter Dorwin Teague and exhibited in the United States Pavilion at the 1939 New York World's Fair.

See page 59.

UPRIGHT TRANSPOSING PIANO, WESER BROTHERS, NEW YORK, serial no. 117728, 1940

National Museum of American History, Smithsonian Institution, gift of Irving Berlin, catalog no. 73.30

88 keys (7 1/3 octaves)

Action:	tape-check upright action
Strings:	copper-wound and plain steel, 1, 2, or 3 strings for each note
Hammers:	felt
Pedals (left to right):	1. soft pedal (moves hammers closer to strings)
	2. transposing mechanism
	3. damper lifter (allows strings to keep vibrating)

Hand lever (under keyboard): moves keyboard and action to allow transposing

Frame:	one-piece cast-iron frame, cross-stringing
Case:	black lacquer

An inscription on the case says "Made expressly for Irving Berlin." The transposing mechanism moves the keyboard and action so that the player can play in any key.

GRAND PIANO, STEINWAY & SONS, MODEL B, NEW YORK, serial no. 367040, 1960
Lent by the Cathedral of St. John the Divine, New York

88 keys (7 1/3 octaves)
Action:	Steinway "accelerated" repetition action
Strings:	copper-wound and plain steel, 1, 2, or 3 strings for each note
Hammers:	felt
Pedals (left to right):	1. una corda (moves hammers to strike 2 of 3 strings)
	2. sostenuto (Steinway patent, lifts selected dampers)
	3. damper lifter (allows strings to keep vibrating)
Frame:	one-piece cast-iron, cross-stringing
Case:	painted white (originally black lacquer over mahogany veneer)

Duke Ellington owned this instrument and used it especially to write sacred music.

See page 57.

MARK I STAGE PIANO, FENDER-RHODES COMPANY, FULLERTON, CA, serial no. 24761, 1971–1973
National Museum of American History, Smithsonian Institution, gift of John Edward Hasse, catalog no. 1988.0047.01

73 keys (6 octaves)
Action:	Rhodes action, hammers facing player
Vibrators:	metal bars with resonator bars and coils to turn vibrations into electrical charges, 1 for each note
Hammers:	rubber pads on plastic shanks
Hand stops above keyboard (left to right):	
	1. tone regulator
	2. volume regulator
Frame:	wood
Case:	wood covered with imitation leather

See page 69.

GRAND PIANO, BALDWIN, MODEL SD-10, CINCINNATI, serial no. 255848 1984
Lent by Baldwin Piano & Organ Company

88 keys (7 1/3 octaves)
Action:	Baldwin repetition action
Strings:	copper-wound and plain steel, 1, 2, or 3 strings for each note
Hammers:	felt
Pedals (left to right):	1. una corda (moves hammers to strike 2 of 3 strings)
	2. sostenuto (lifts selected dampers)
	3. damper lifter (allows strings to keep vibrating)
Frame:	one-piece cast-iron frame, cross-stringing
Case:	wood encrusted with Austrian rhinestones, inside of lid covered with a mirror

The instrument was made for and used by Liberace, American television and recording pianist.

See page 71.

DX-7 ELECTRONIC KEYBOARD, YAMAHA, HAMAMATSU, JAPAN, serial no. 82395, 1986
National Museum of American History, Smithsonian Institution, gift of Yamaha Corporation of America, catalog no. 2000.0261.01

Action:	keys activate pressure-sensitive switches for instrumental sounds programmed on microchips
Case:	plastic

See page 69.

See page 63.

DISKLAVIER UPRIGHT PIANO, YAMAHA, HAMAMATSU, JAPAN, serial no. 5243713, 1988

National Museum of American History, Smithsonian Institution, gift of Yamaha Corporation of America, catalog no. 1990.3132.02

88 keys (7 1/3 octaves)

Action:	Yamaha upright action
Strings:	copper-wound and plain steel, 1, 2, or 3 strings for each note
Hammers:	felt
Pedals (left to right:	1. soft pedal (moves hammers closer to strings)
	2. moderator (moves felt between hammers and strings to mute sound)
	3. damper lifter (allows strings to keep vibrating)
Frame:	one-piece cast-iron frame, cross stringing
Case:	polyurethane lacquered wood, Plexiglas front panel

The Disklavier system is an electronic reproducing system, recording to a floppy disk.

See page 69.

TRITON ELECTRONIC KEYBOARD, KORG, MELVILLE, NY, serial no. 9204, 1999

National Museum of American History, Smithsonian Institution, gift of Korg USA, Inc., catalog no. 2000.0262.01

Action:	keys activate pressure-sensitive switches for instrumental sounds programmed on microchips.
Case:	plastic.

See page 69.

XP-80 ELECTRONIC KEYBOARD, ROLAND CORPORATION, HAMAMATSU, JAPAN, serial no. CM68253, 1999

National Museum of American History, Smithsonian Institution, gift of Roland Corporation U.S., catalog no. 2000.0263.01

Action:	keys activate pressure-sensitive switches for instrumental sounds programmed on microchips.
Case:	plastic.

See page 67.

GRAND PIANO, PRO2000, YAMAHA, HAMAMATSU, JAPAN, serial no. 5872002, 2000

National Museum of American History, Smithsonian Institution, gift of Yamaha Corporation of America, catalog no. 2000.0273.01

88 keys (7 1/3 octaves)

Action:	Yamaha repetition action
Strings:	Wound and plain steel, 1, 2, or 3 strings for each note
Hammers:	felt
Pedals (left to right):	1. una corda (moves hammers to strike 1 or 2 strings)
	2. sostenuto (lifts selected dampers)
	3. damper lifter (allows strings to keep vibrating)
Frame:	one-piece cast-iron aluminized frame, cross-stringing
Case:	cherry and brushed aluminum, lid Plexiglas in two sections

In addition to all the parts of a piano, the instrument features computer-based control of the keys. A monitor displays musical scores and an educational guide system turns pages. Its player mechanism can record to CDs. It also has a DVD player, voice control, and the ability to play music from a CD or an external video.

Between 1890 and 1920, H.O. Studley, who worked in the Poole piano factory in Quincy, Massachusetts, created this masterpiece of a tool chest from factory scraps, including ivory, ebony, mahogany, and mother of pearl. The chest ingeniously organizes more than 300 tools and would have hung near Studley's workbench.

Courtesy of Robert Gilson, SI photograph by Eric Long.